Name: Date:

Cutting Skills

Color the triangles and cut along the dashed lines.

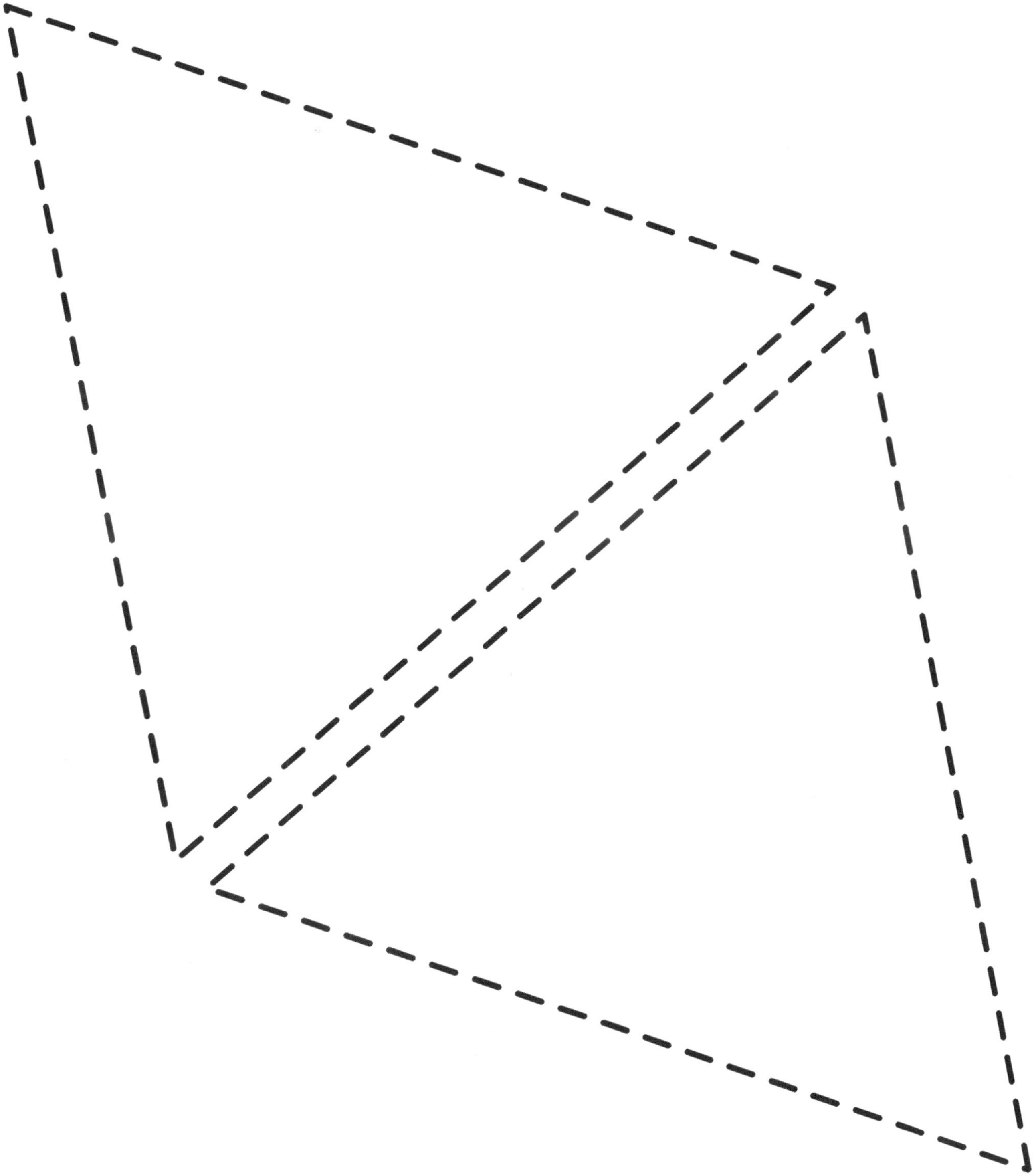

Cutting Skills

Color the inverted trapezoid and cut along the dashed lines.

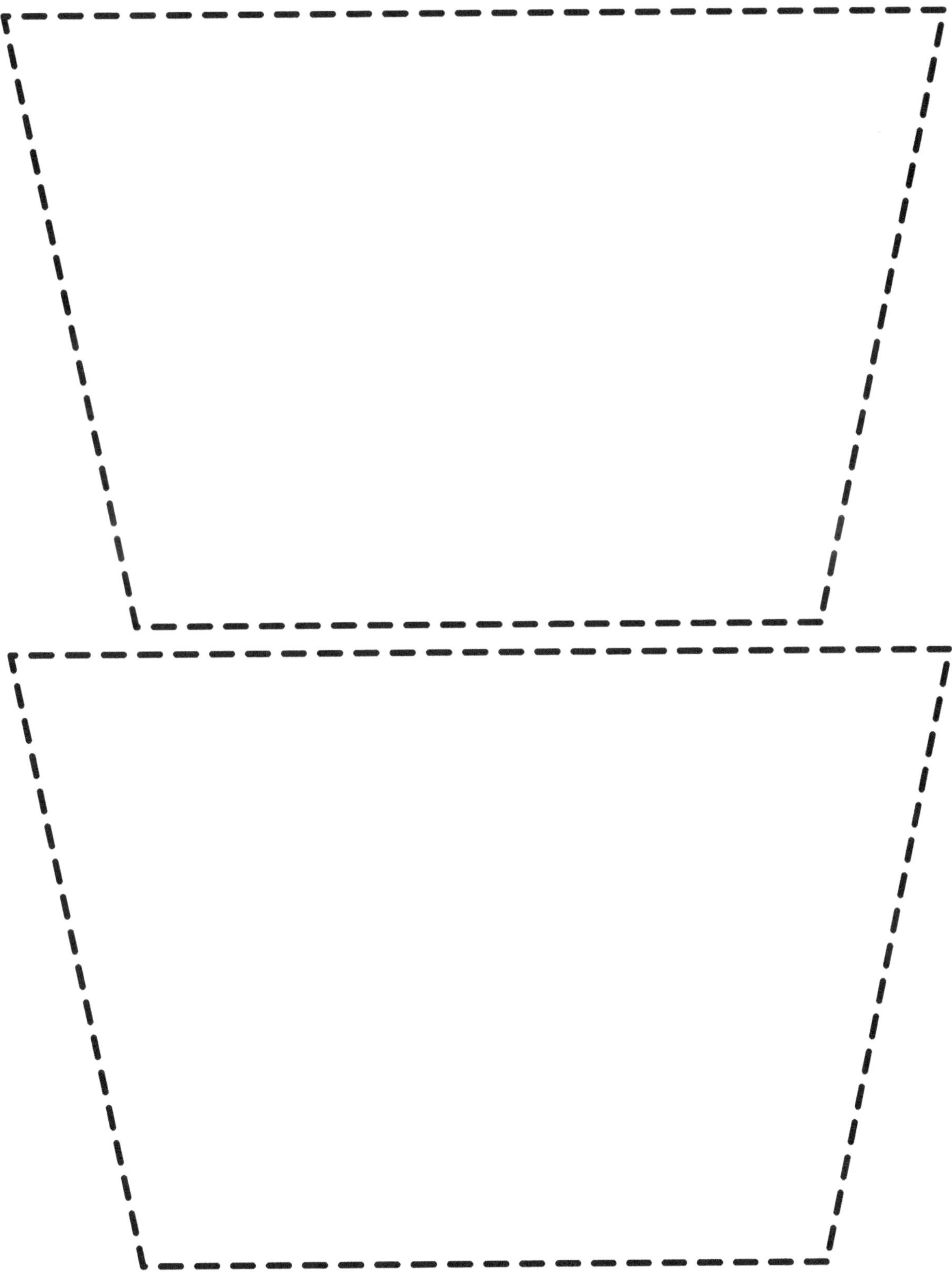

Cutting Skills

Color the triangles and cut along the dashed lines.

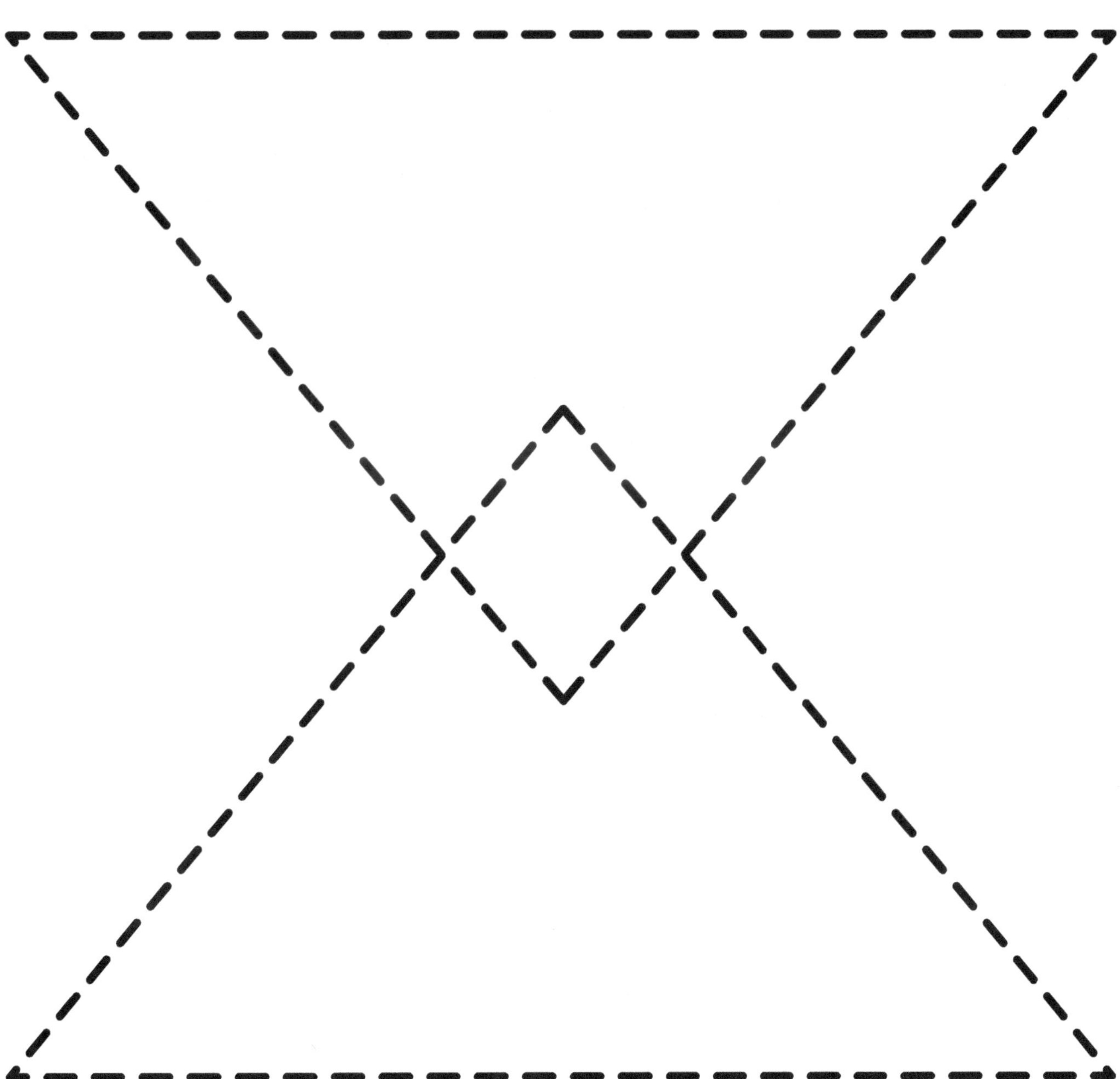

Cutting Skills

Color the circles and cut along the dashed lines.

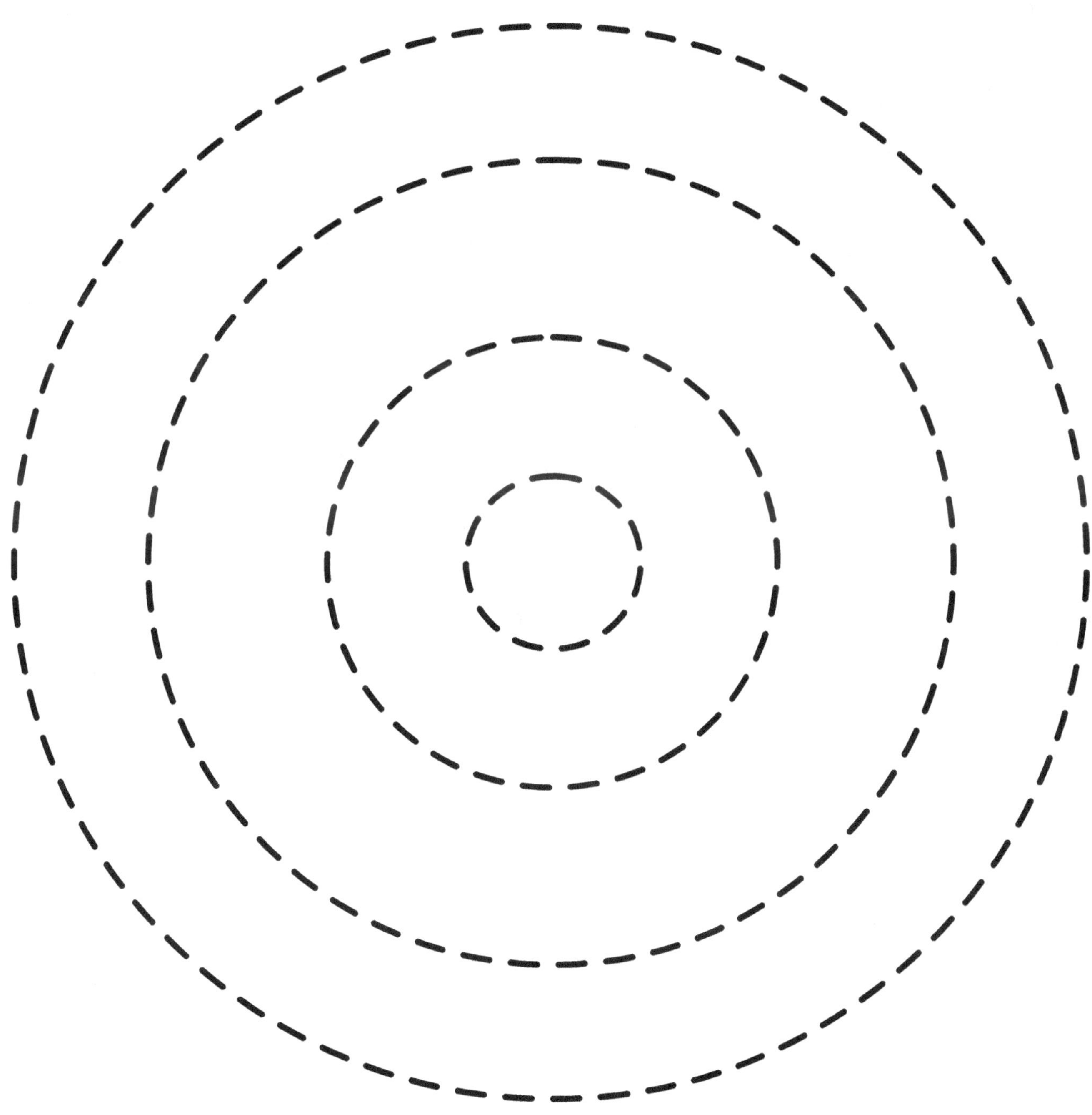

Cutting Skills

Color the star and cut along the dashed lines.

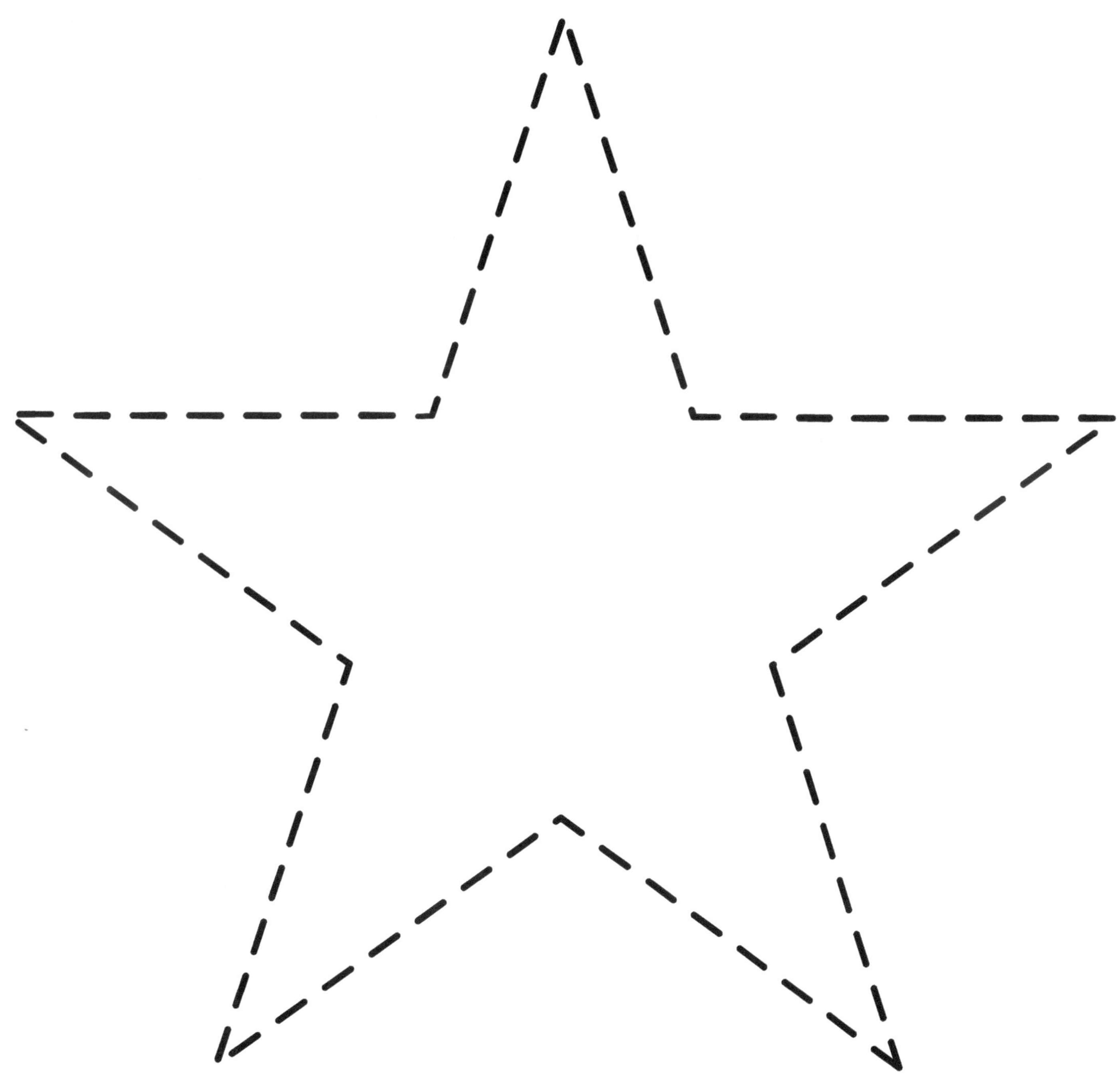

Cutting Skills

Color the flags and cut along the dashed lines.

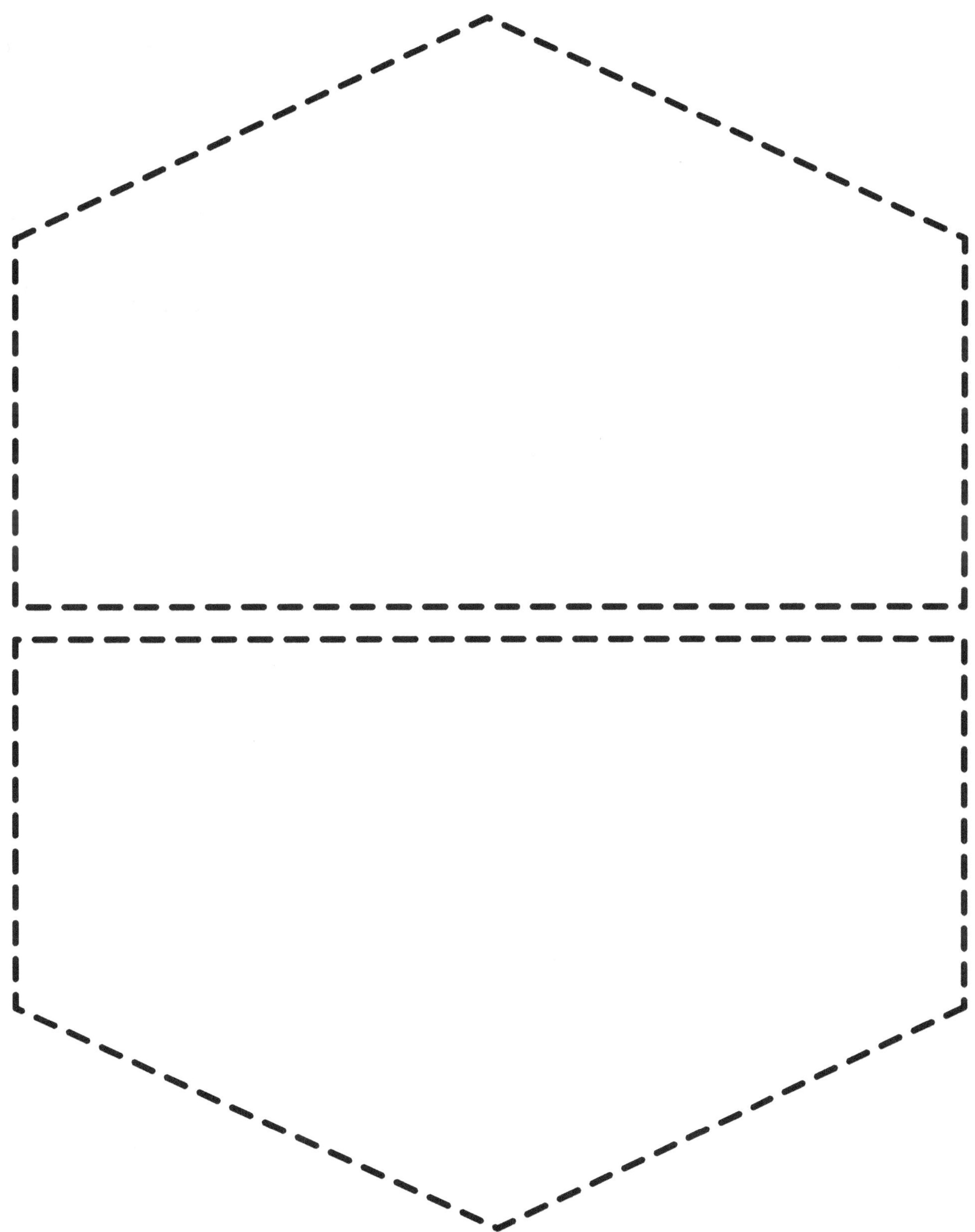

Cutting Skills

Color the arrows and cut along the dashed lines.

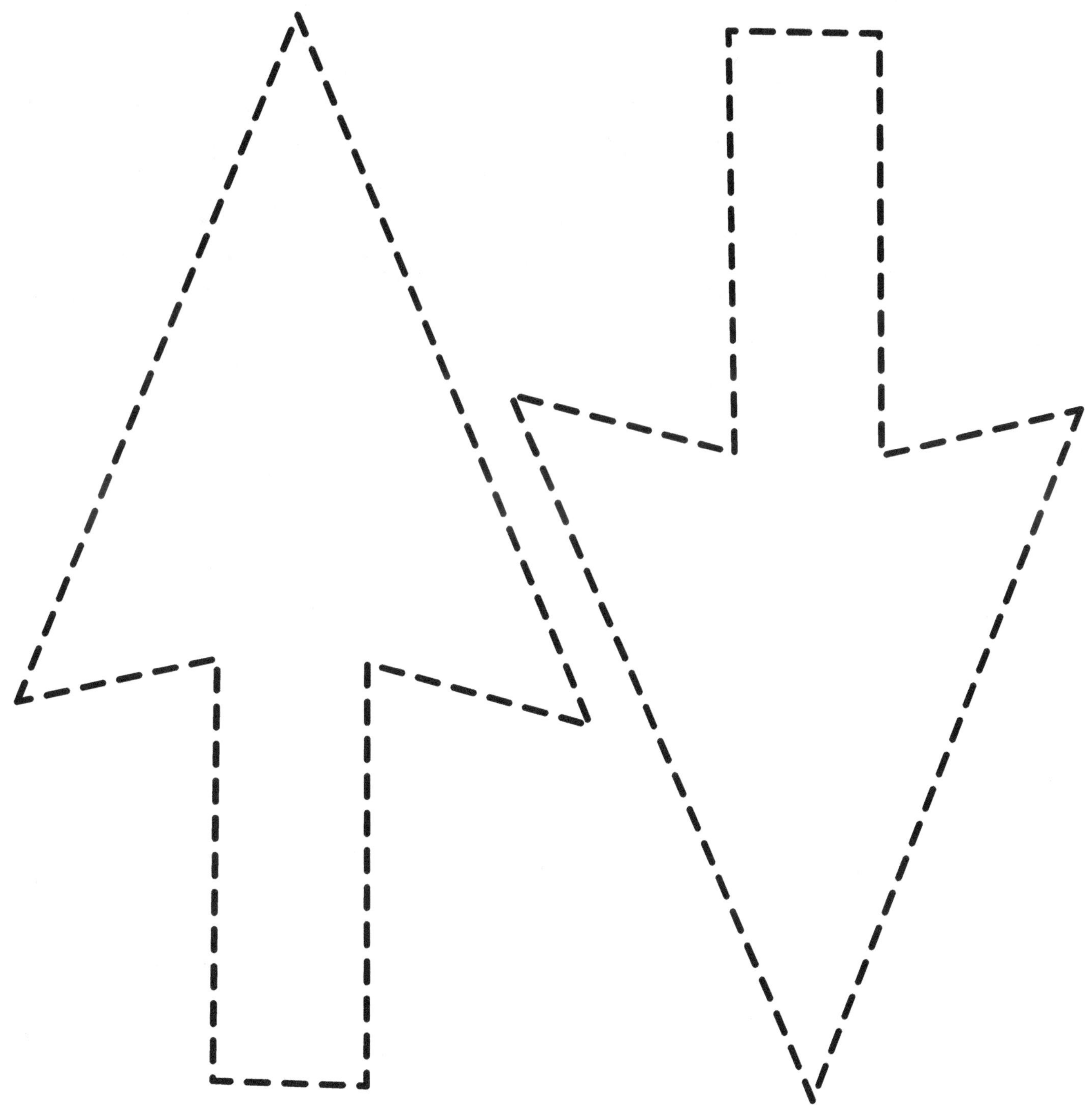

Cutting Skills

Color the hexagon and cut along the dashed lines.

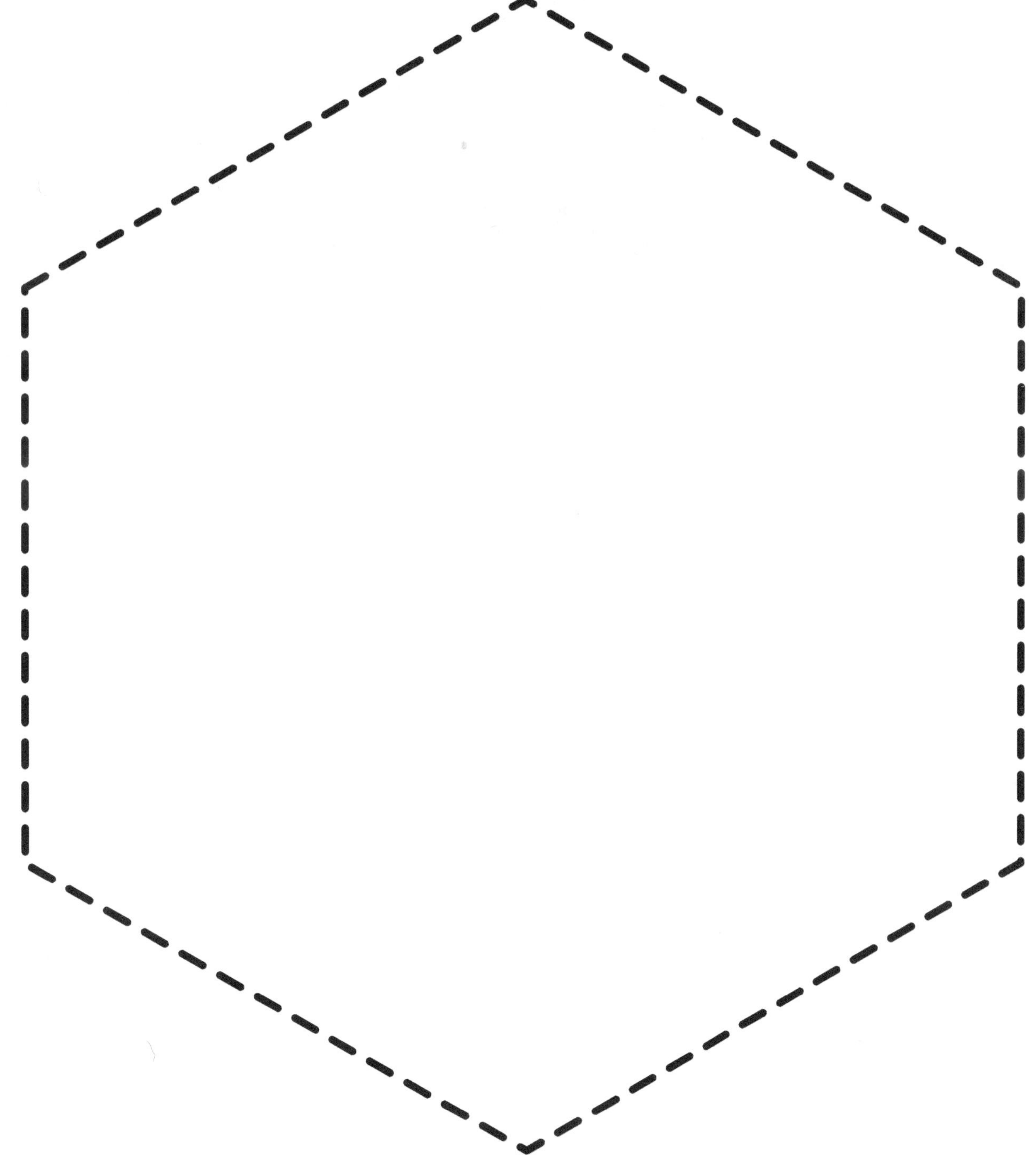

Cutting Skills

Color the stamp and cut along the dashed lines.

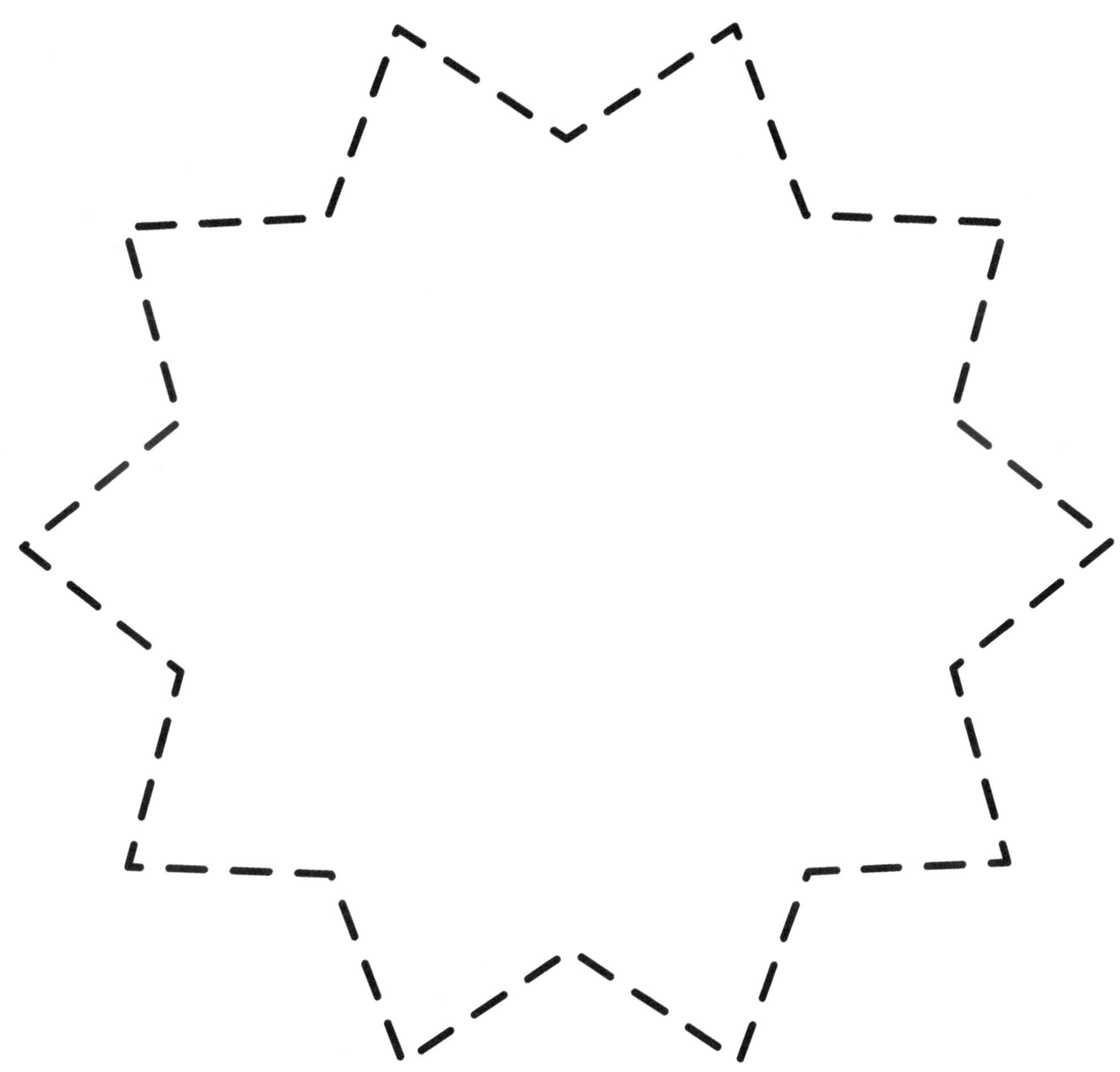

Cutting Skills

Color the plane and cut along the dashed lines.

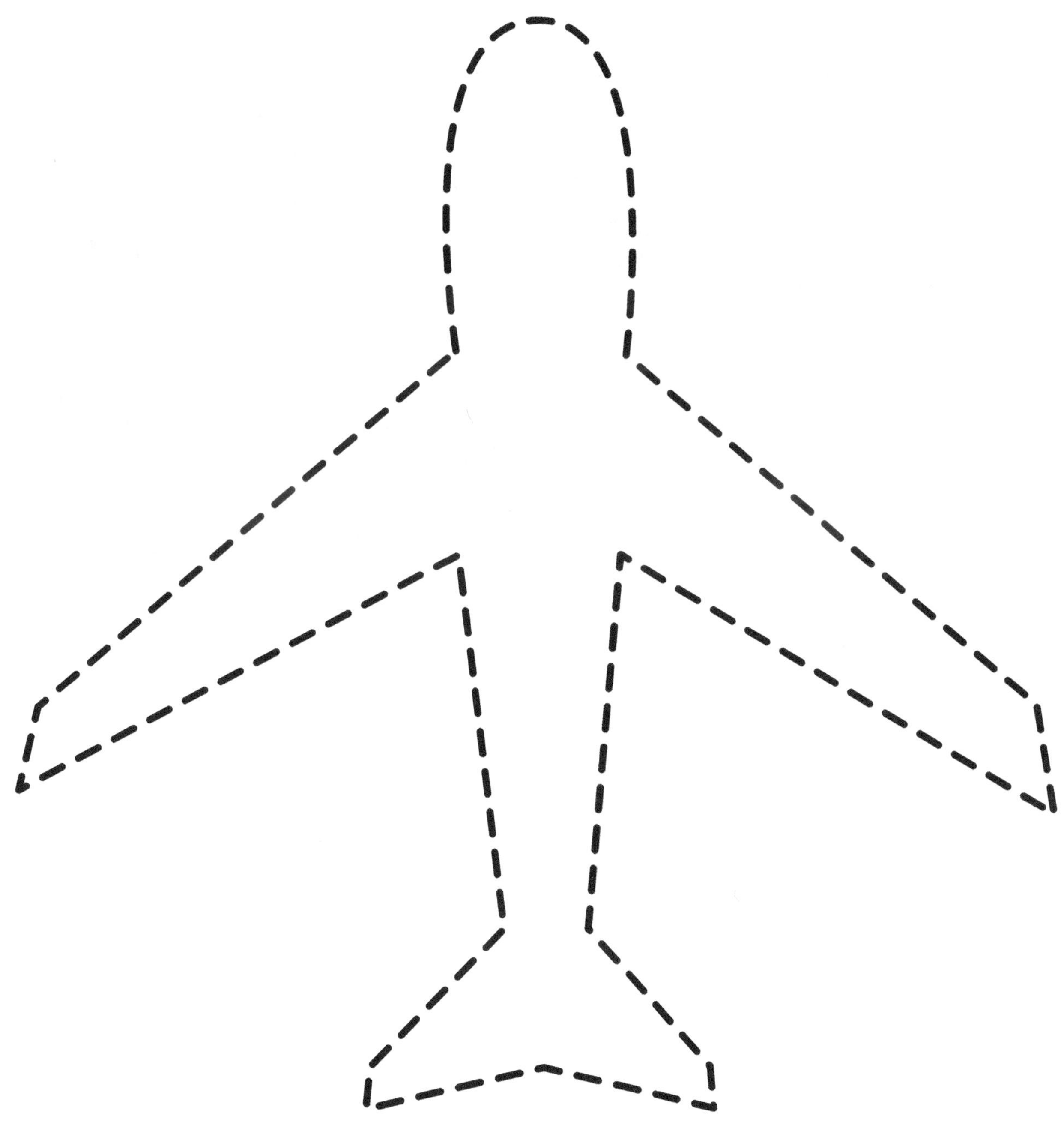

Cutting Skills

Cut along the dashed lines.

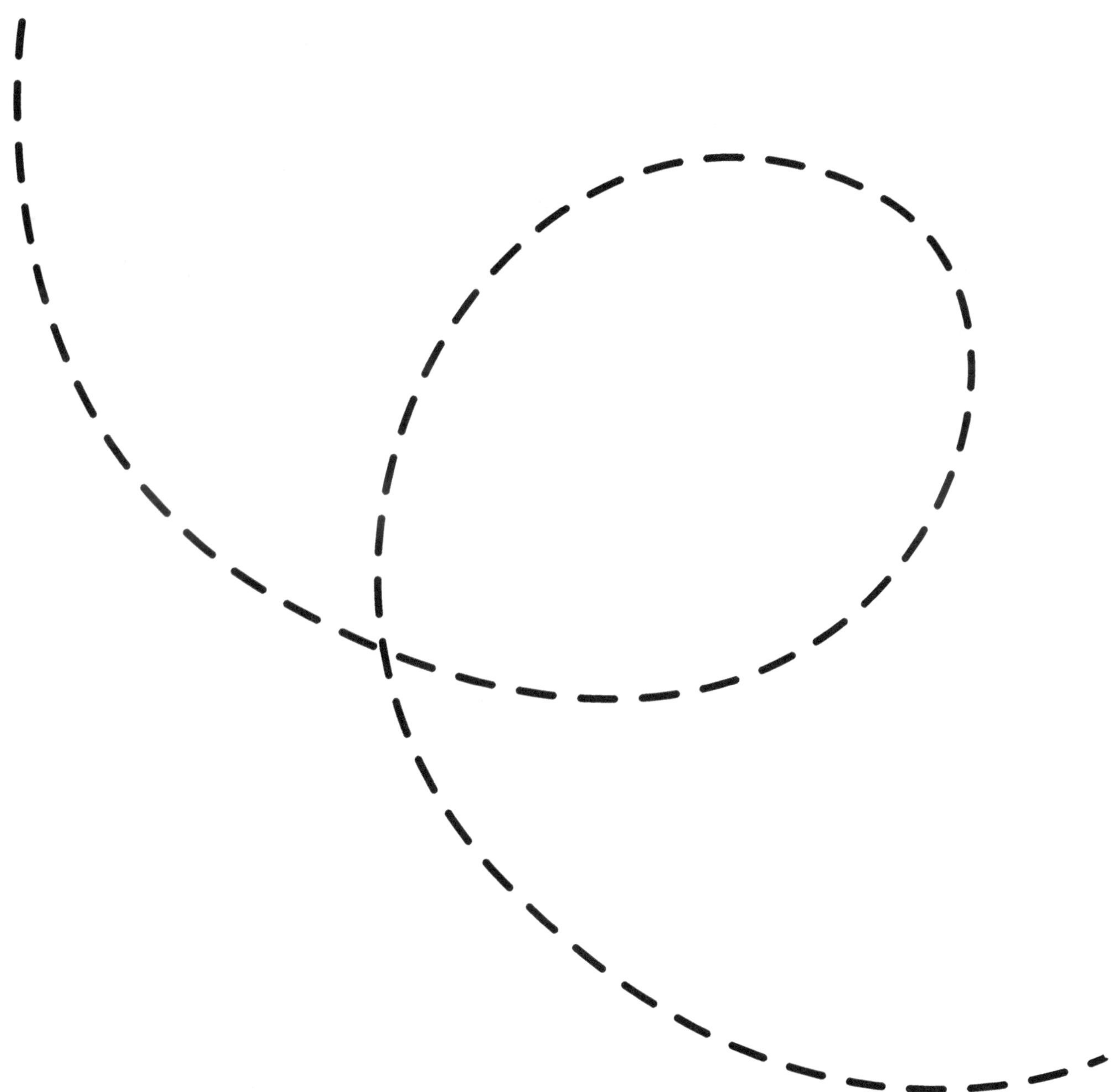

Cutting Skills

Color in the cute cats and cupcakes. Cut along the dashed lines.

Cutting Skills

Color in the sea elements and cut along the dashed lines.

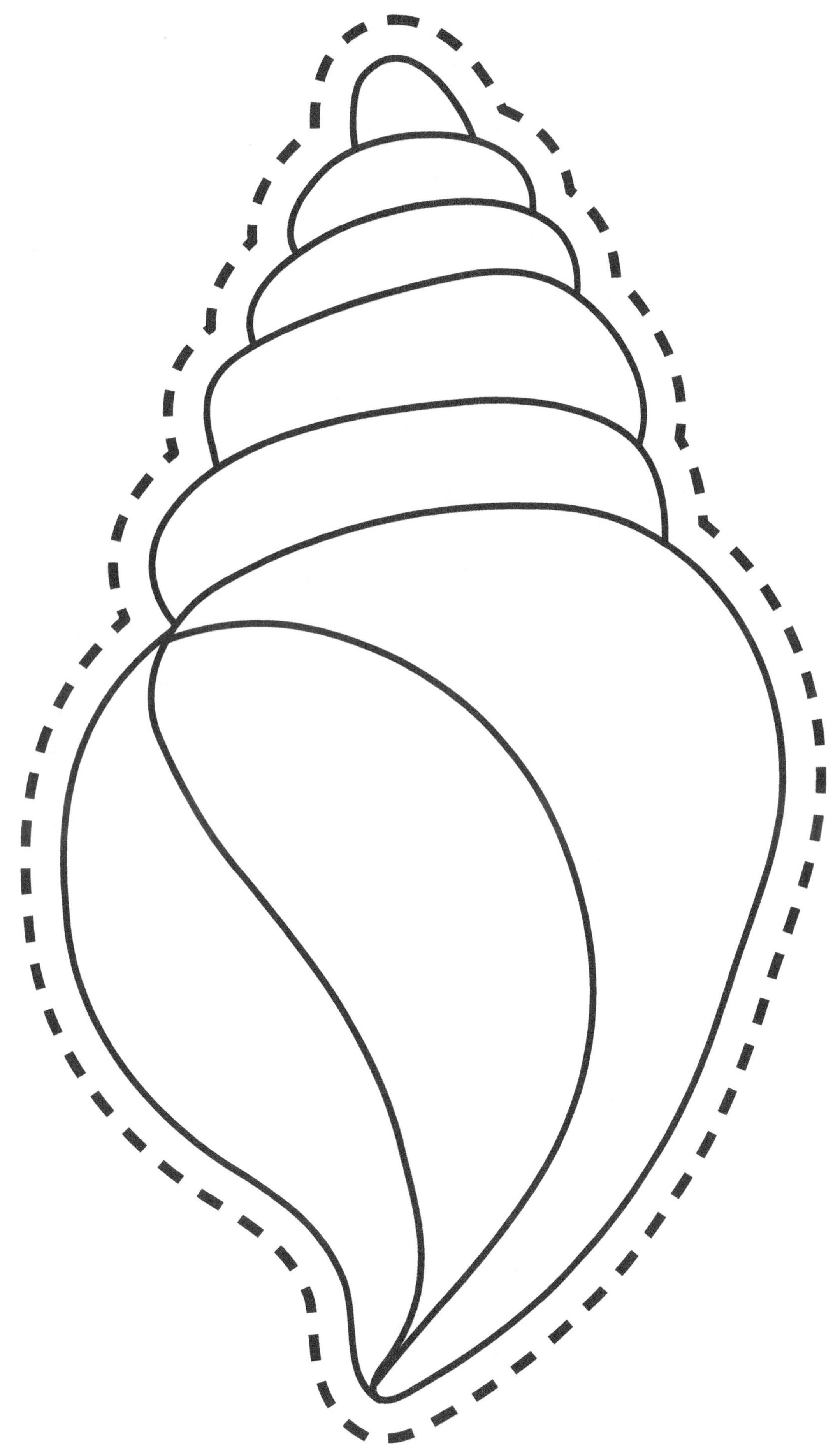

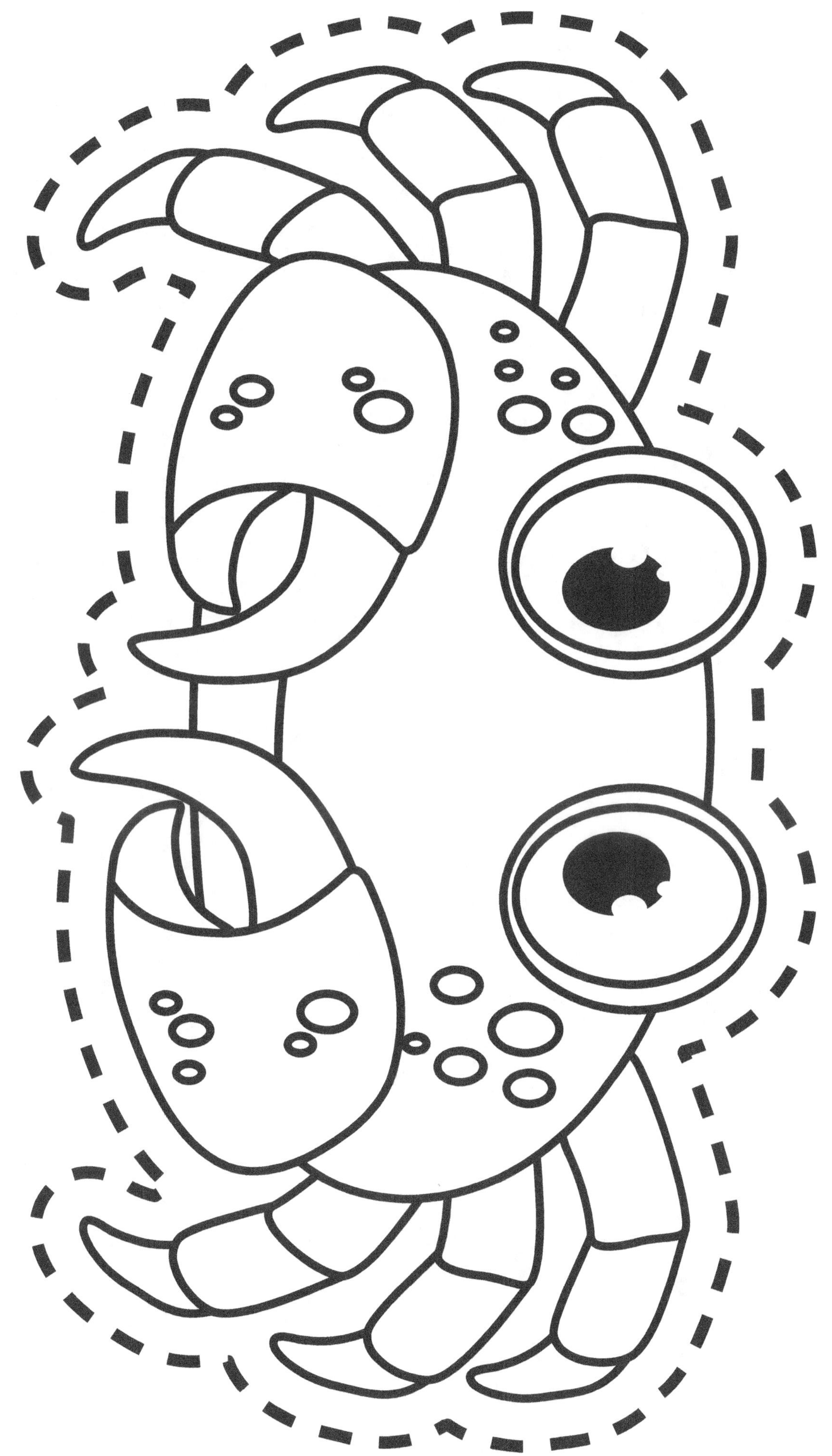

SCISSOR SKILLS

Carefully practice your scissor skills cutting from the bottom to the stop sign.

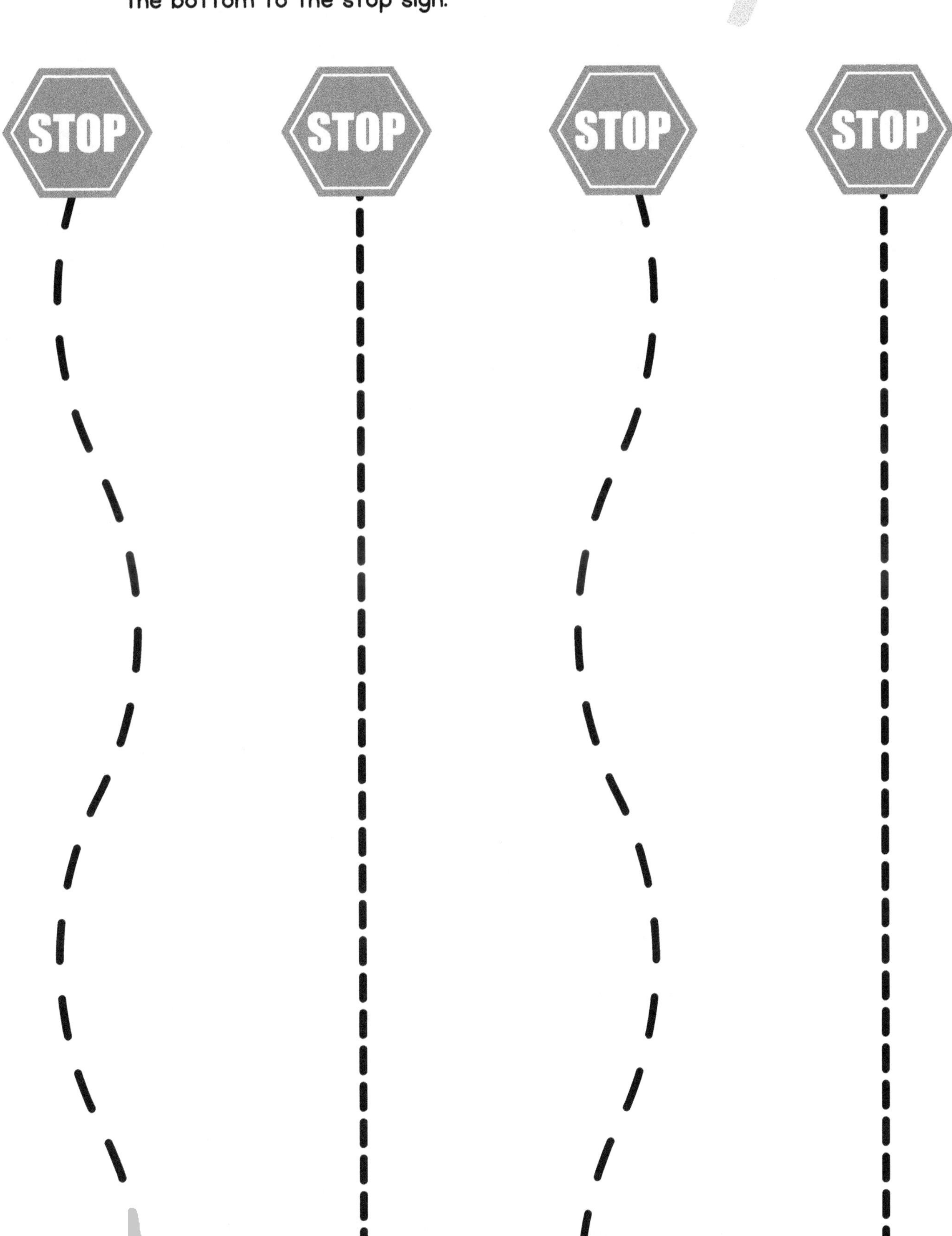

SCISSOR SKILLS

Practice your cutting skills by cutting on the dotted line up to the crayon.

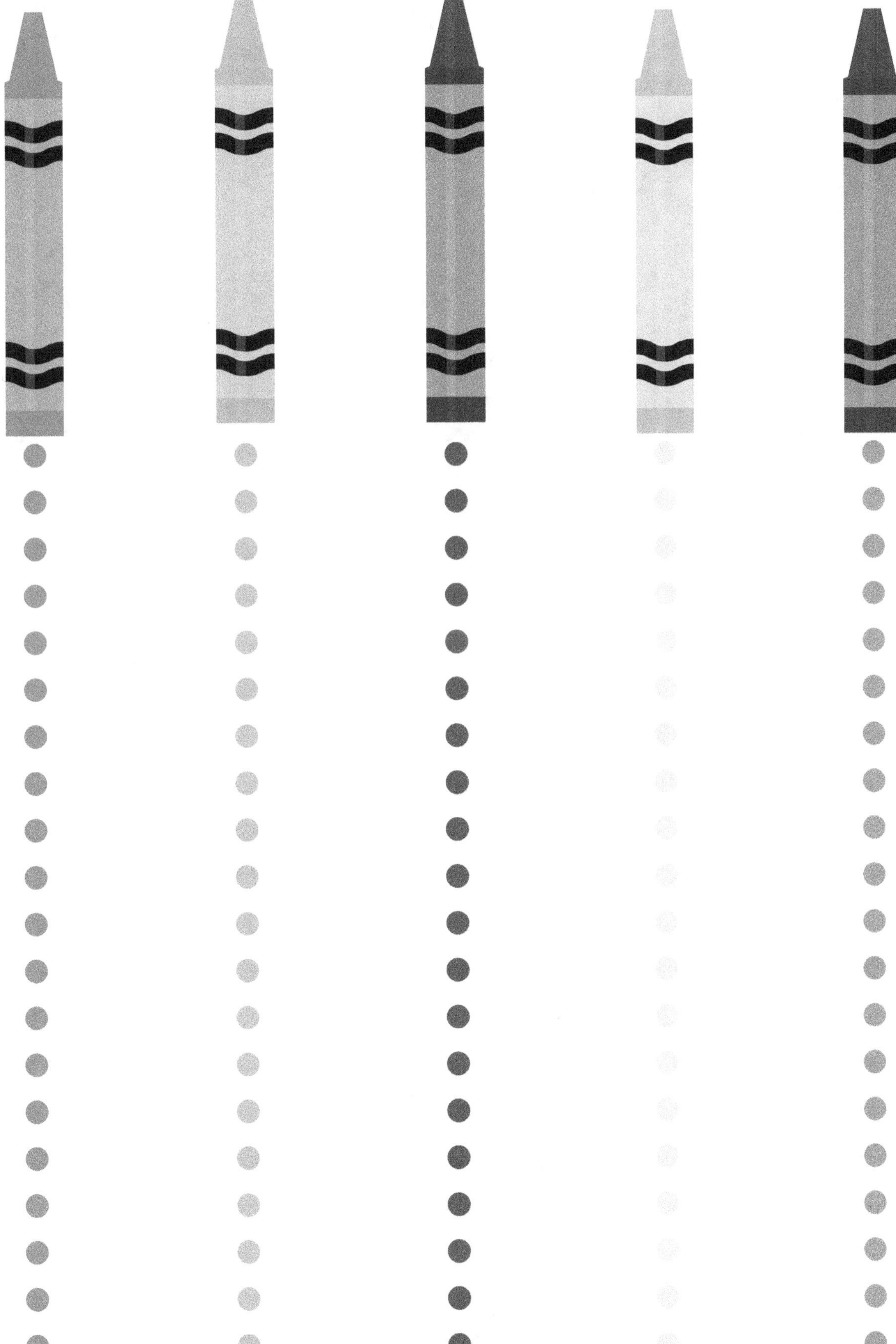

Name:

SCISSOR SKILLS

Carefully practice your scissor skills cutting from the bottom to the school supplies shown.

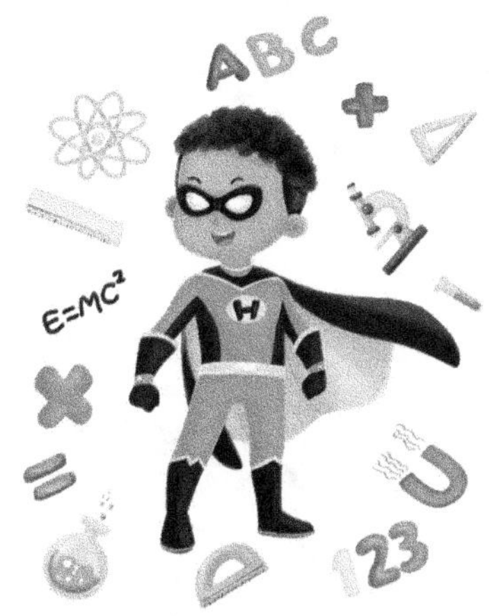

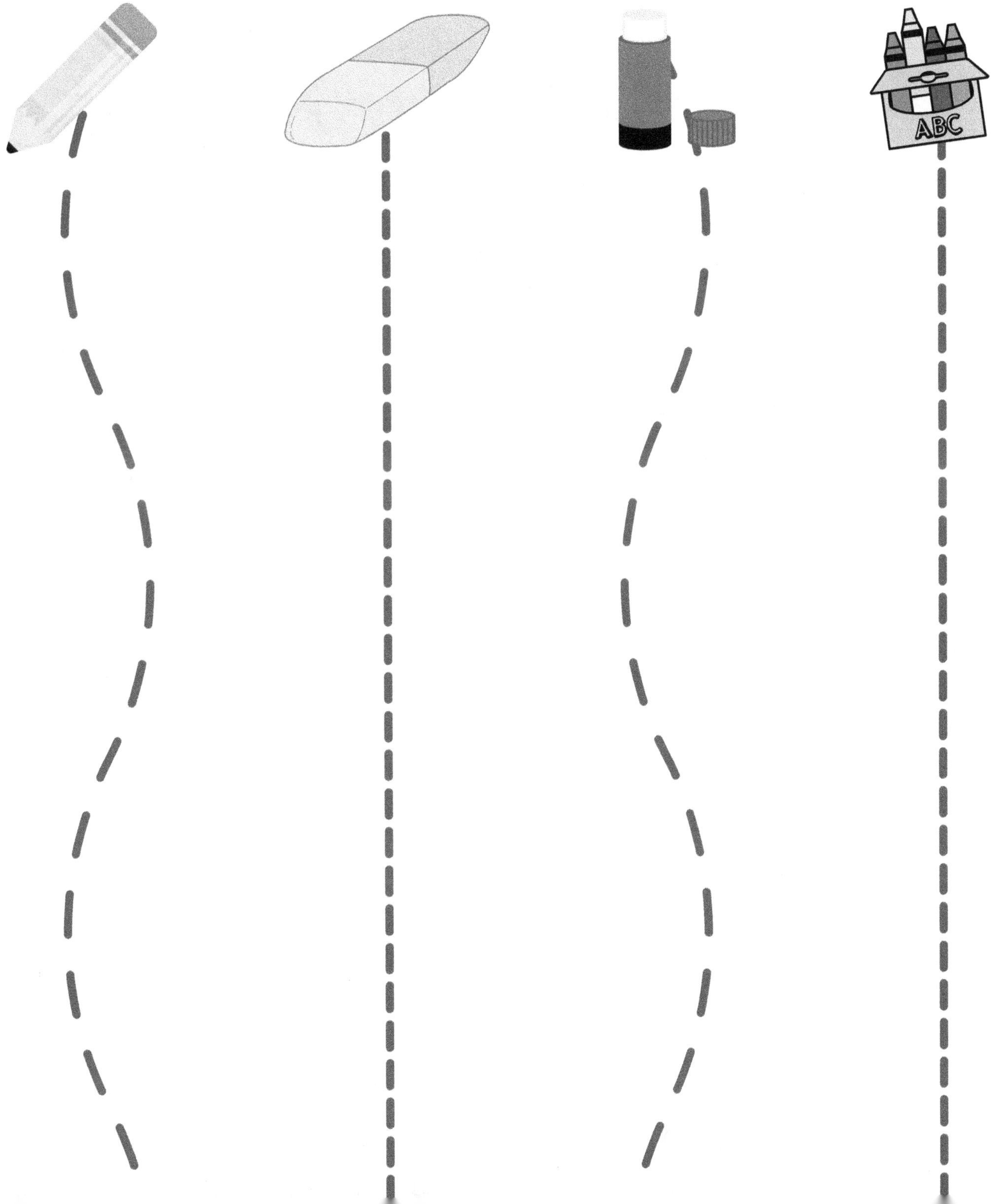

HELP CUPID

Help Cupid get to the hearts by carefully cutting from the bottom of the page to the hearts.

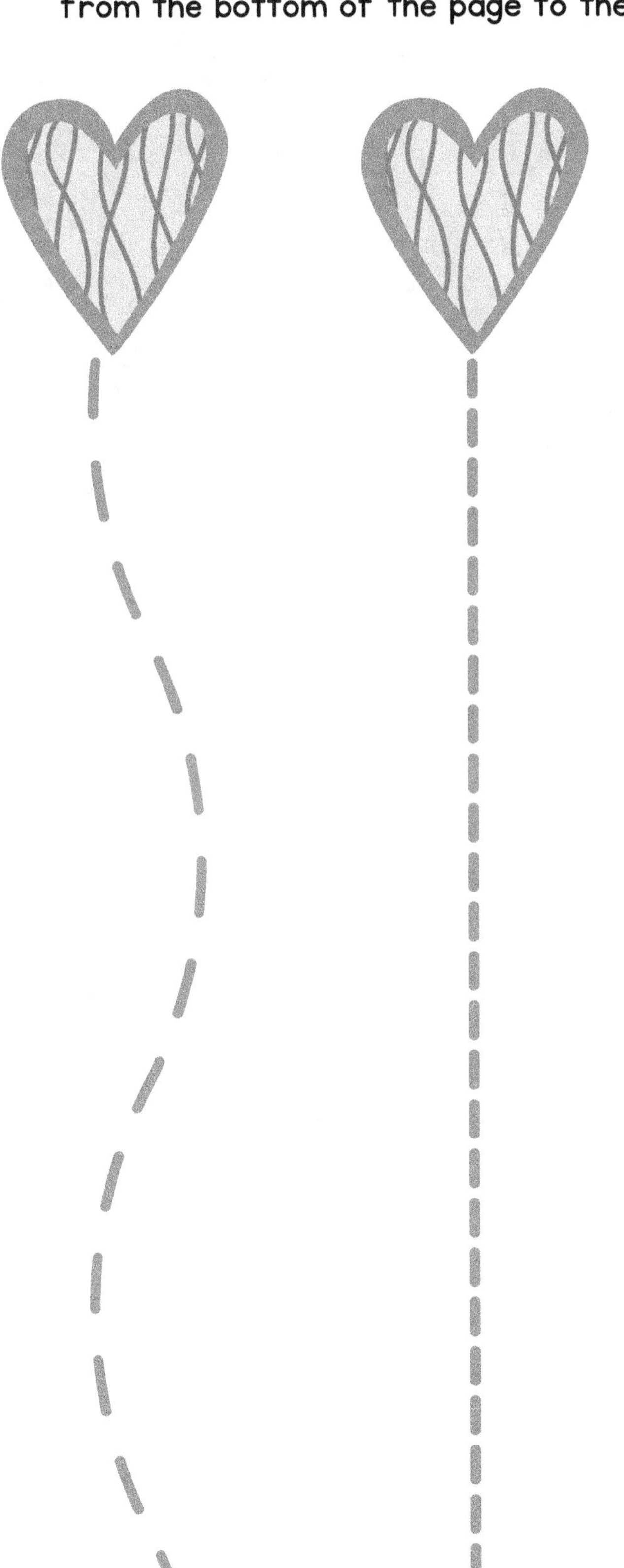

Name:

SCISSOR SKILLS

Carefully practice your scissor skills cutting from the bottom to the pumpkins.

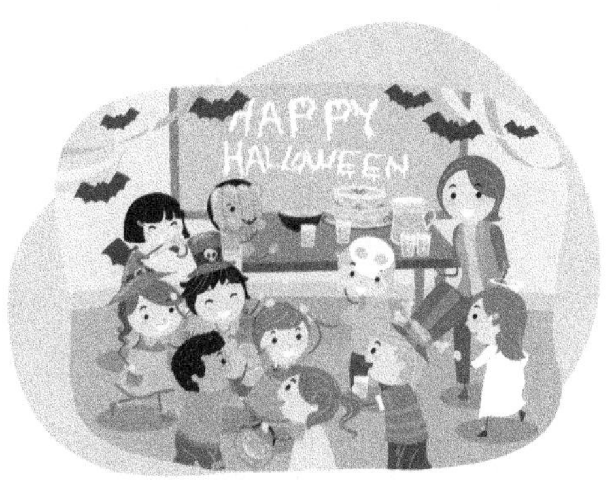

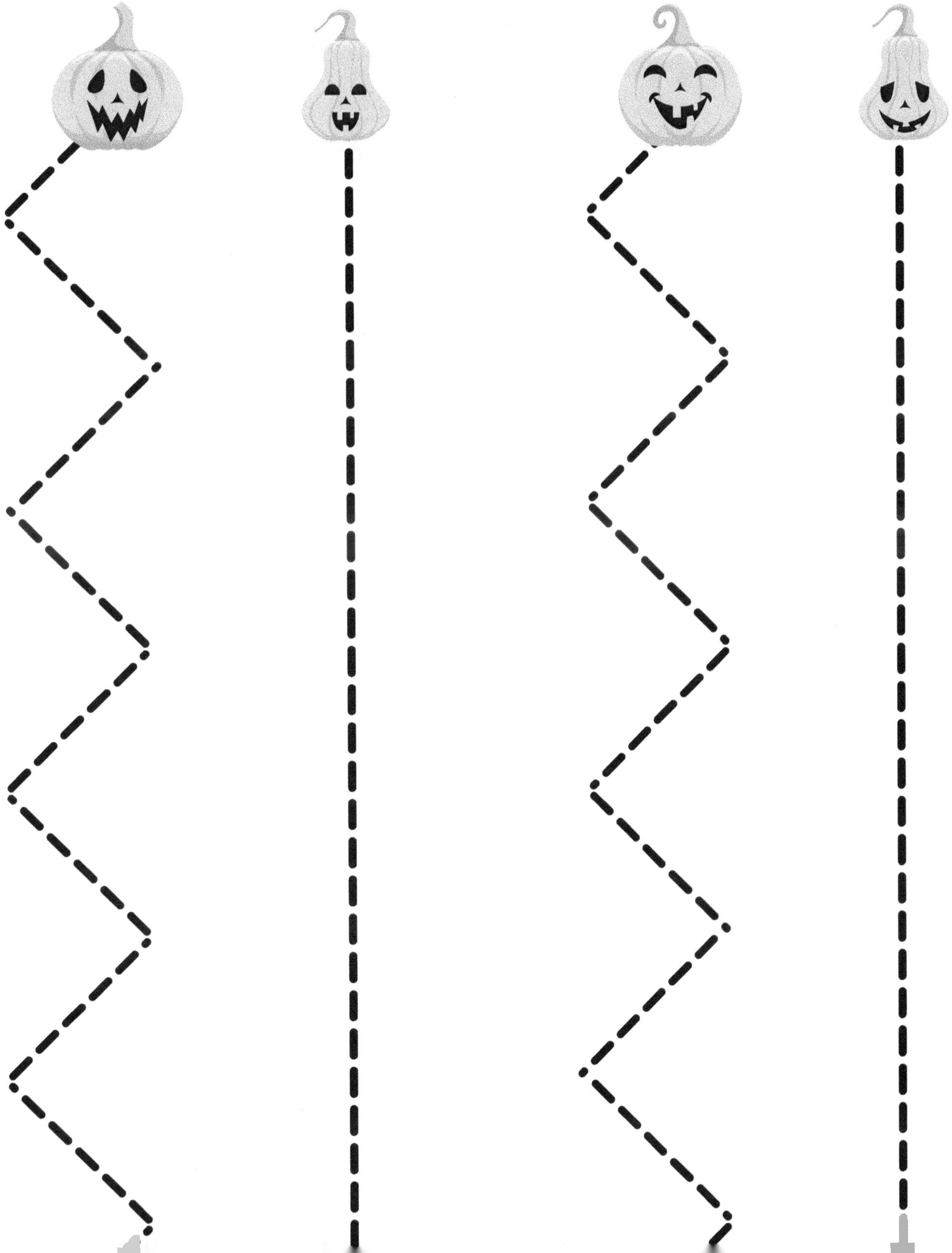

Name:

SCISSOR SKILLS

Carefully practice your scissor skills cutting from the bottom to the pumpkin pies! Tom the Turkey cannot wait to taste this pie!

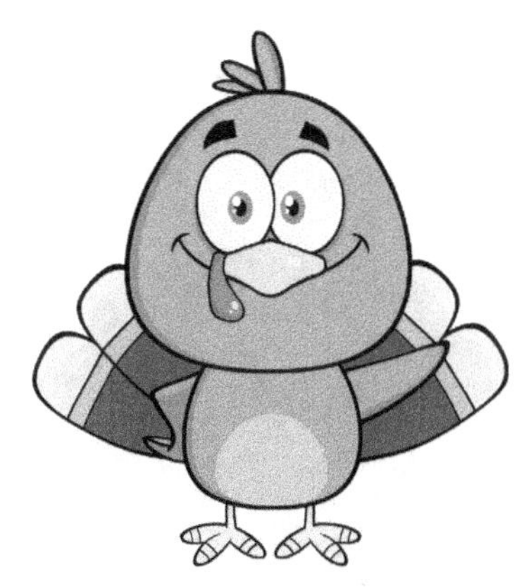

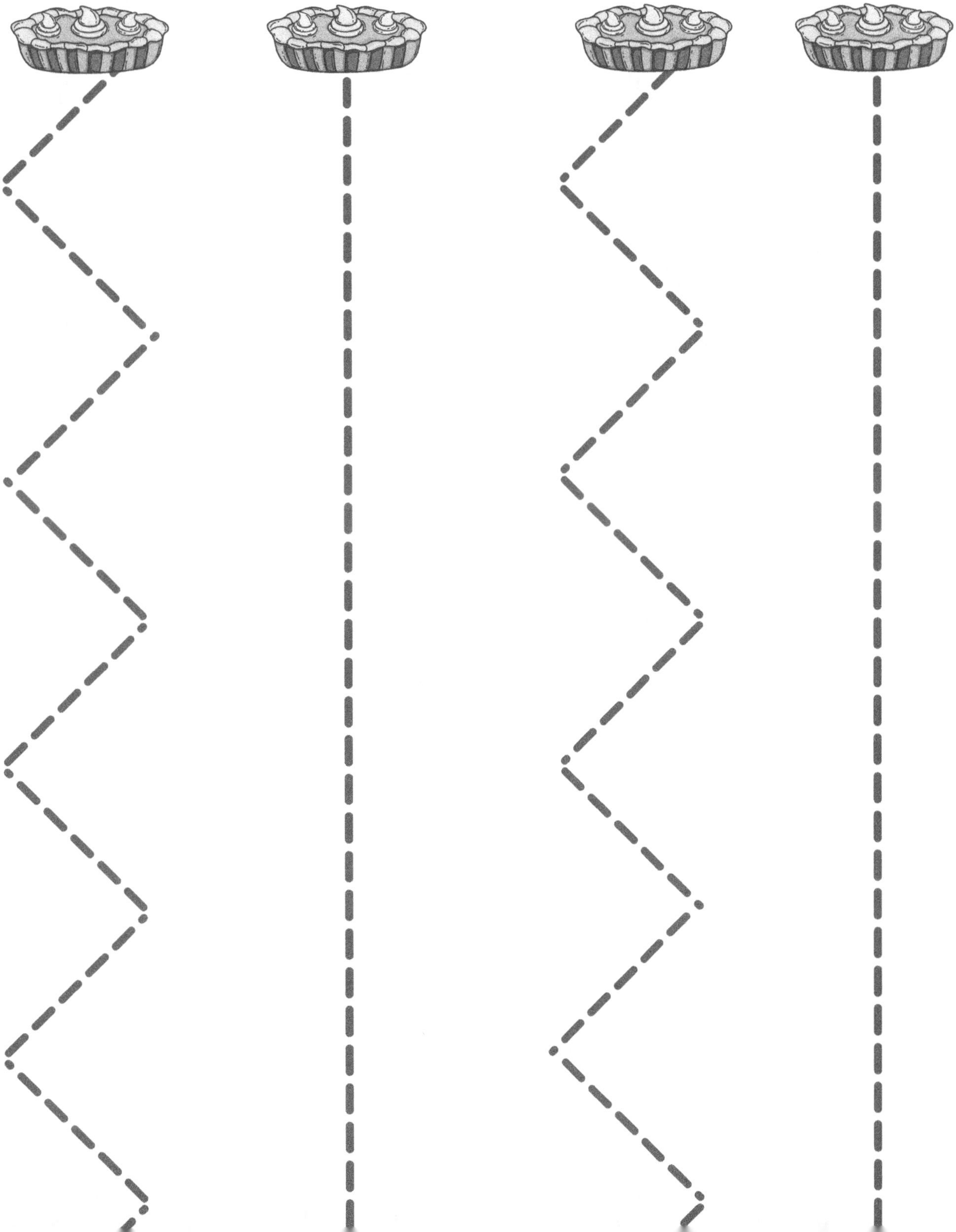

CHRISTMAS GIFT SCISSOR SKILLS

Carefully practice your scissor skills cutting from the bottom to the Christmas gifts!

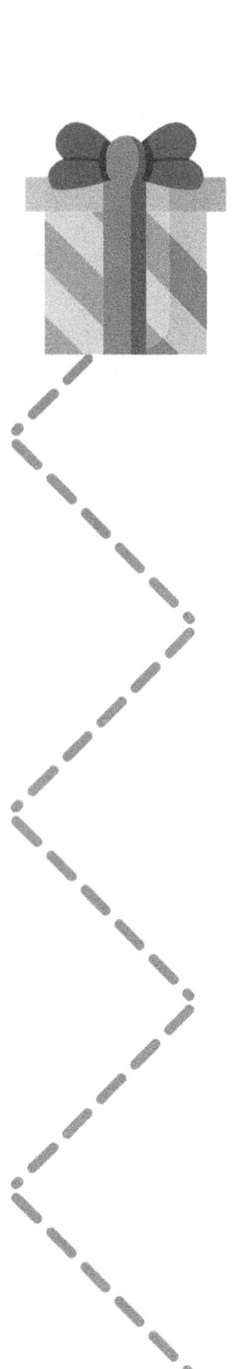